T0087008

Vaughan Williams for Choirs 2

JOHN LEAVITT

10 secular pieces compiled and arranged for accompanied and unaccompanied mixed voices

MUSIC DEPARTMENT

OXFORD
UNIVERSITY PRESS

OXFORD
UNIVERSITY PRESS

Great Clarendon Street, Oxford OX2 6DP,
United Kingdom

Oxford University Press is a department of the University of Oxford.
It furthers the University's objective of excellence in research, scholarship,
and education by publishing worldwide. Oxford is a registered trade mark of
Oxford University Press in the UK and in certain other countries

This collection © Oxford University Press 2020

John Leavitt has asserted his right under the Copyright, Designs
and Patents Act, 1988, to be identified as the Editor of this anthology

First published 2020

Impression: 1

All rights reserved. No part of this publication may be reproduced,
stored in a retrieval system, or transmitted, in any form or by any means,
without the prior permission in writing of Oxford University Press

Permission to perform the works in this anthology in public
(except in the course of divine worship) should normally be obtained
from the Performing Right Society Ltd (PRS) at www.prsformusic.com
or a local performing right licensing organization, unless the owner or the
occupier of the premises being used already holds a licence from such an
organization. Likewise, permission to make and exploit a recording must
be obtained in advance from the Mechanical-Copyright Protection
Society Ltd (MCPS) at www.prsformusic.com or a local mechanical
copyright licensing organization

Enquiries concerning reproduction outside the scope of the above should be
directed to the Music Rights Department, Oxford University Press, at
music.permissions.uk@oup.com or at the address above

ISBN 978-0-19-353209-0

Music and text origination by Andrew Jones
Printed in Great Britain on acid-free paper by
Halstan & Co. Ltd, Amersham, Bucks.

Contents

Preface	iv
Notes on the pieces	v
Spring	9
The Singers	14
An Invitation	21
Whether men do laugh or weep	27
John Dory	36
Nothing is here for tears	45
She's like the swallow	49
Greensleeves	52
Silence and Music	58
Land of our birth	67

Preface

Welcome to this collection of new arrangements of short choral pieces by one of the finest British composers of the twentieth century. Born in 1872 in Gloucestershire, Ralph Vaughan Williams attended the Royal College of Music and read history and music at Trinity College, Cambridge. He studied composition with C. Hubert H. Parry and Charles Villiers Stanford, and received further tuition overseas from Max Bruch and Maurice Ravel. After a distinguished career, producing a particularly wide-ranging catalogue of works, Vaughan Williams died on 26 August 1958. His ashes were interred at Westminster Abbey.

Vaughan Williams's various musical activities—from choir master, editor, and folk-song collector to composer and conductor—greatly enhanced British musical life; but they also contributed to a mistaken view that his original composition was in some way parochial, designed for domestic consumption. He believed in the value of music education, and wrote pieces for amateurs and service music for the church; but he also displayed great sensitivity to the twentieth-century human condition, projecting a message of peace and reconciliation in works such as *Dona Nobis Pacem* (1936). Moreover, he wrote works of great artistic integrity and imagination that have stood the test of time, not least for choirs, and for all levels of music making.

Vaughan Williams was inspired by great literature and by a lifelong belief that the voice 'can be made the medium of the best and deepest human emotion' (*Vaughan Williams on Music*, ed. D. Manning, Oxford, 2007). Made up of two volumes and organized into sacred and secular works, the current collection is designed to introduce new generations of choral conductors and choirs to Vaughan Williams, sharing his music's variety and timeless quality. There is a mix of familiar and unfamiliar titles. A second aim was to make the pieces, where necessary, match today's scoring and performance needs, improving accessibility and extending their usefulness in a way that would have appealed to Vaughan Williams. At one extreme the arrangements have new piano parts for unaccompanied sections, for example, to lend support, or contain small judicious cuts. Others are arranged in a friendlier key (taking into account the range, also), or for SATB choir from a unison or treble-voice original—the subject matter and content lending itself equally well to adults. At the other end, pieces were selected for their ongoing appeal and suitability, requiring no more than light editorial amendments. In all cases, the harmony, words, and dynamics are unaltered, and my aim has been to respect the integrity and spirit of the original work.

The following commentary, on individual pieces, specifies the changes, sources, and possible uses in performance.

Finally, I wish to record my thanks to Oxford University Press for assisting my research and allowing access to its extensive catalogue, and to The Vaughan Williams Charitable Trust for its kind support.

John Leavitt
2019

Notes on the pieces

Spring from Three Children's Songs
Source: '1. The Singers', OUP, 1930
Suggested programming: Spring concert

This piece, originally written for unison chorus and piano, has been arranged for mixed choir. The piano pedal should be used modestly and according to the harmonic changes in the piece.

The Singers from Three Children's Songs
Source: '2. The Singers', OUP, 1930, renewed in the USA, 1958
Suggested programming: Spring concerts

This piece, originally written for unison chorus and piano, has been arranged for mixed choir. This rhythmic piece requires energetic diction, especially in the softer sections. The piano should be played mostly secco but pedal may be used in places such as bars 17 to 23.

An Invitation from Three Children's Songs
Source: '3. An Invitation', OUP, 1930
Suggested programming: Spring concerts

This piece, originally written for unison chorus and piano, has been arranged for mixed choir. The piano should play mostly secco but pedal may be used in sections such as bars 10 and 12.

Whether men do laugh or weep
Source: 'Whether Men Do Laugh or Weep', OUP, 1931
Suggested programming: Festival or general concert

Changes have been made to the piano layout to facilitate better efficiency between the hands. The piano pedal should be used modestly so as not to blur the musical lines, and should not be used at all in the section with a staccato left hand bass.

John Dory
Source: 'John Dory', OUP, 1934
Suggested programming: General concerts or encores

Changes have been made to the piano layout to facilitate better efficiency between the hands. The piano part is for rehearsal only.

Nothing is here for tears
Source: 'Nothing is here for tears' for SA chorus and piano, OUP, 1936
Suggested programming: Funeral, commemoration, or patriotic concert

This piece has been arranged for SATB voices and piano. The unison vocal parts between bars 4 and 30 have been divided between the contrasting sections of the choir (Sopranos/Tenors and Altos/Basses), and arranged for four-part singing in bars 33–40. Changes have been made to the piano layout for efficiency, and the piano pedal should be used sparingly to avoid blurring the musical lines.

She's like the swallow
Source: 'She's Like the Swallow', Oxford Choral Songs (unison and piano), OUP, 1934
Suggested programming: General concerts

This folksong was originally arranged for unison voices with piano accompaniment. Here, it is rearranged for unaccompanied SATB voices with a soloist. The choral parts conform to the harmonic structure of the original piano part.

Greensleeves
Sources: 'Greensleeves', Vaughan Williams Collected Songs, Vol. 1, OUP, 1934; 'Greensleeves', Oxford Choral Songs (SA and piano), OUP, 1954; 'Greensleeves' for SATB a cappella, OUP, 1945
Suggested programming: Spring or Autumn concerts

An accompanied SATB arrangement of this piece has been created from three sources by Vaughan Williams: a version for solo voice and piano, a version for SA and piano, and an a cappella version for SATB voices. The harmony of the SATB chorals conforms to the original harmonic structure of the piano parts taken from the two accompanied editions. The piano pedal may be used modestly.

Silence and Music
Source: 'Silence and Music', OUP, 1953, renewed in the USA, 1955
Suggested programming: General concert

This piece originates from a cycle of songs for mixed voices entitled, 'A Garland for the Queen': a collection of pieces by ten British composers to mark the occasion of the Coronation of H.M. Queen Elizabeth II. Changes have been made to the piano layout to facilitate better efficiency between the hands. The piano part is for rehearsal only.

Land of our birth

Sources: 'Land of Our Birth' for unison and piano, OUP, 1945; 'A Song of Thanksgiving', OUP, 1945

Suggested programming: Festival or patriotic concert

This arrangement for SATB chorus and piano has been created from two sources: a version for unison voices and piano, and 'A Song of Thanksgiving'. The first three verses draw from the unison version. Verse four then segues into the SATB setting from 'A Song of Thanksgiving' before returning to the unison anthem for the final verse. In this verse, this arrangement mirrors the choral parts from 'A Song of Thanksgiving' to conform with the unison anthem piano part. The vocal parts in bars 54–7 draw upon both settings of the piece. The piano pedal may be used modestly throughout.

Spring

from 'Three Children's Songs'

Frances M. Farrer
(1895–1977)

RALPH VAUGHAN WILLIAMS (1872–1958)
arr. John Leavitt

Duration: *c.*2 mins

© Oxford University Press 1930 & 2020. Words reprinted by kind permission.

6
bathed in sun;
oo
T.
B.
Down by the brook the wil - lowslean And
9
When Au - tumn with a
in and out the chil - dren run;
12
Then
gold - en train Steps forth in all her proud ar - ray, oo

farm - ers work with might and main
15
To stack the har - vest.
18
safe a - way.
p
21
p (sotto voce)
Win - - ter stark And
unis. p
When Win - ter fol - lows stark and cold And

24
all the land is wrapped, Then beasts
all the land is wrapped in sleep, Then beasts be-gin to
27
pp
seek And birds to shel - ter creep.
pp
seek their fold And birds to warmth and shel - ter creep.
pp
31
mf
But when at last comes
mf
mf

Then
34
smil - ing Spring, And birds and beasts a - wake once more, oo
must we all for glad - ness sing,
37
For Spring holds hap - pi -
40
pp
rit.
- ness in store.
mm
pp
rit.
pp

The Singers

from '*Three Children's Songs*'

Frances M. Farrer
(1895–1977)

RALPH VAUGHAN WILLIAMS (1872–1958)
arr. John Leavitt

Duration: *c.*2 min

© Oxford University Press 1930 & 2020. Words reprinted by kind permission.

7
S./A.
unis.
mp
But what shall we be?
O, we will sing high
T./B.
unis.
mp
and
mp
11
And no - thing on earth shall pre - vent us, A
we will sing low,
14
mf
fig for your in - dus - try, off you may go, 'Tis sing - - -
mf
mf
Ped.

17
- ing, 'tis sing - - - - - ing, 'tis
Ped.
20
f
sing - ing a - lone shall con - tent us.
f
f
25
Sam will drive a bus,
S. p
B. p
Sue will be a dress-mak- er,
p

28
S./A. unis.
A.
p
Har - ri - et will keep a shop, But what of all us?
T.
p
T./B. unis.
mp
O,
32
mp
and we will sing low, And no - thing on earth shall pre -
(mel.)
we will sing high
35
(mel.)
- vent us, A fig, in - dus - try, off, go, 'Tis
A fig for your in - dus - try, off you may go,

38
sing - - - ing, 'tis sing - - - ing, 'tis
Ped.
Ped.
42
f
sing - ing a - lone shall con - tent us.
f
f
47
unis. p
E - li - za - beth, Tom, Har - ri - et, John and Sam and Sue,
unis.
p
p

50
mp
O,
Though you have a trade in store
O, won't you sing too?
O,
mp
mp
54
we will sing high
mp
and we will sing low,
And no-thing on earth shall pre-
we will sing high
mp
and we will sing low,
57
-vent us, A fig for your in-dus-try, off you may go, 'Tis

60
f
sing - - - ing,
'tis
'tis sing - - - ing,
f
Ped.
Ped.

64
rit.
sing - ing a - lone shall con - tent us.
rit.
f

An Invitation

from 'Three Children's Songs'

Frances M. Farrer
(1895–1977)

RALPH VAUGHAN WILLIAMS (1872–1958)
arr. John Leavitt

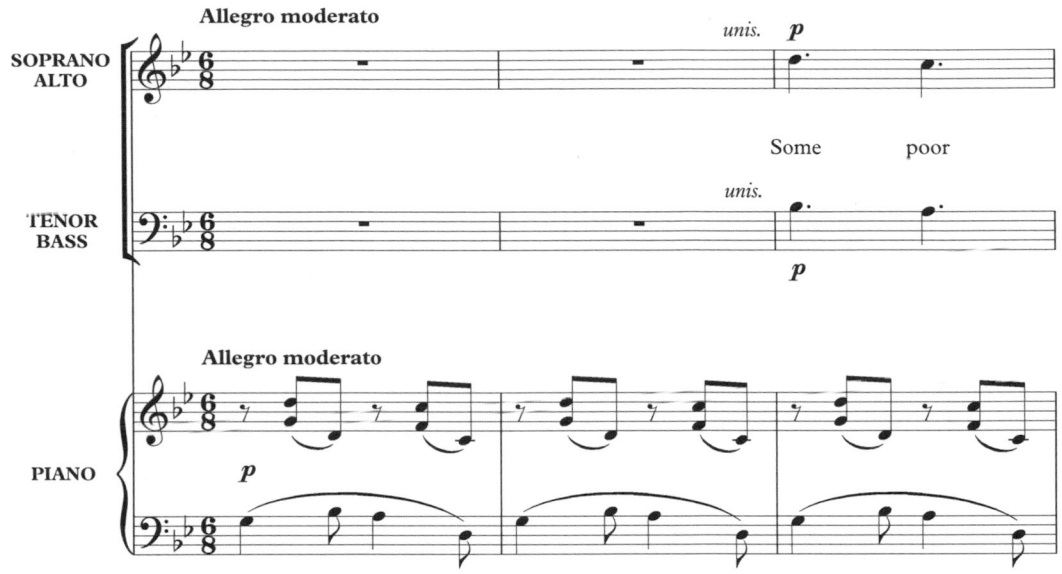

Duration: *c.*3 mins

© Oxford University Press 1930 & 2020. Words reprinted by kind permission.

7
S.
A.
grass turns brown, And there's ne - ver a morn - ing black-bird to sing
T.
B.
10
rall.
a tempo
Out - side their win-dow to tell them of Spring.
rall.
a tempo
p
13

16
p
unis.
T.
B.
Pi - ty poor fel - lows who live in the town, Where the
19
gri - my smuts come tum - bling down; Here in the coun - try the
22
rall.
gen - tle rain Wash - es us clean and fresh a -

a tempo
25
- gain.
mp
28
S.
A.
mp
They say that the fel - lows who live in the town
31
Work so hard that they fret and they frown; What a mis - take when
rit.
a tempo
34
they could be free And hap - py like us in the o - pen coun - try.
f

37
S.
A.
unis. f
So come, poor fel - lows, and leave your dull
T./B.
unis.
f
40
p
towns,
Leave your
p
Come to the Val - leys, come to the Downs,
p
43
mo - ney bags, leave your wealth,
Come and find hap - pi - ness, strength and

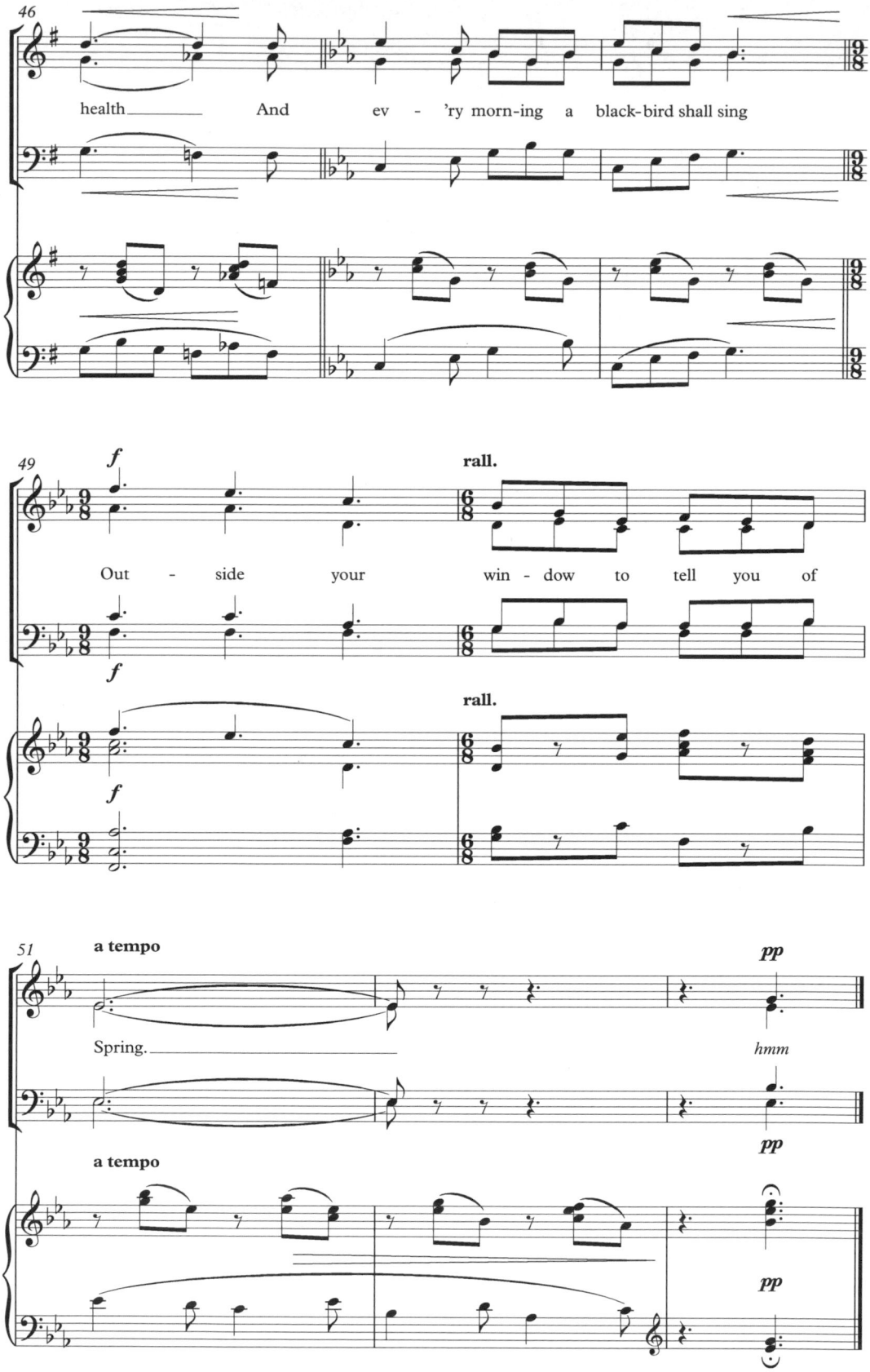
46
health And ev - 'ry morn-ing a black-bird shall sing
49
f
rall.
Out - side your win - dow to tell you of
f
rall.
f
51
a tempo
pp
Spring.
hmm
pp
a tempo
pp

Whether men do laugh or weep

Words from
Campion and Rosseter's *Book of Airs* (1601)

RALPH VAUGHAN WILLIAMS (1872–1958)
ed. John Leavitt

Duration: *c.*3 mins

© Oxford University Press 1931 & 2020.

16
There is un-der-neath the sun no-thing in true earn - - - - est
p
20
S.
mf
There is un - der-neath the sun no - thing in true
A.
mf
There is un - der - neath the sun no - thing
T.
mf
done, there is un - der - neath the sun
B.
mf
done, there is no - thing, there is no - thing un - der-neath the

23
f
earn - - est done, in true earn - - - - -
in true earn - est done. Whe-ther men do
no-thing in true earn - - est done. Whe-ther men do
sun in true earn - est done. Whe-ther men do
p
27
mf cresc.
- est done, there is un-der-neath the sun
laugh or weep, Whe-ther they do wake or sleep, Whe-ther they die
mf

earn - - - - - - - -
ff
31
no-thing in true earn - est, no - thing in true earn -
young or old, Whe-ther they feel heat or cold, There is un-der-neath the
young or old, Whe-ther they feel heat or cold, There is un-der-neath the
young or old, Whe-ther they feel heat or cold, There is un-der-neath the
- est, in
35
unis.
- est, in true earn - est done.
sun no-thing in true earn - - - est done.
sun no-thing in true earn - - - est done.
sun no-thing in true earn - - - est done.

40
45
S.
All our pride is but a jest.
A.
T.
None are worst and none are best.
B.
None are worst and none are best.
sub. p
49
Grief and joy and hope and fear Play their pa - geants
Play their pa - geants ev - 'ry -

53
p
Vain o - pin - ion all doth sway, And the world,
ev - 'ry - where. Vain o - pin - ion all doth sway, And the
p
All doth sway, And the world is
- where. Vain o - pin - ion all doth sway, And the
57
cresc.
f
S.1
and the world is but a play, and the
cresc.
f
S.2
the world is but a play, and the world is but a
cresc.
f
A.
world is but a play, is but a play, and the world
cresc.
f
T.
but a play. Whe-ther men do laugh or weep, Whe-ther they do
cresc.
f
B.
world is but a play. Whe-ther men do laugh or weep, Whe-ther they do
cresc.
f marc.

* First sopranos may join second sopranos for the bracketed passage, in which case altos sing the small notes.

69
and the world is but a play.
and the world is but a play.
and the world is but a play.
- - - - est done.
- - - - est done.
73
S.
ff
And the world,
A.
ff
And the world,
T.
ff
And the world,
B.
ff
And the world,
ff

77
and the world is but a
and the world is but a
and the world is but a
and the world is but a
82
play.
play.
play.
play.

John Dory

English folksong
arr. RALPH VAUGHAN WILLIAMS (1872–1958)
ed. John Leavitt

Duration: *c.*3 mins

© Oxford University Press 1934 & 2020.

7
Do - ry bought him an am - bling nag To Pa - ris for to
Do - ry was fit - ted, the por - ter was wit - ted To let him in there -
mf
tide - a, a tide - a a a, To
gate - a, the gate - a a a, there -
tide - a, a tide - a a a, To
gate - a, the gate - a a a, To
tide - a, a tide - a a a, To
gate - a, the gate - a a a, To
10
ride - a, to Pa - ris for to ride - a, to
-at - a, to let him in there - at - a, to
ride - a, to Pa - ris for to ride - a, to
-at - a, to let him in there - at - a, to
mf
Pa - ris for to ride, to ride - a, to
let him in there - at, there - at - a, to
mf
Pa - ris for to ride, to ride - a, to
let him in there - at, there - at - a, to

13
1.
2.
Pa - ris for to ride - a.
let him in there - - at, up - on a ho - ly
pp
Pa - ris for to ride - a, to
let him in there - - at, up - on a ho - ly
f
Pa - ris for to ride - a, to
let him in there - - at.
3. The
Pa - ris for to ride - a, to
let him in there - - at.
3. The
16
mf
tide - - - a.
King
tide - - - a.
King
first man that John Do - ry did meet Was good King John of
(4.) par - don, a par - don, my liege and king, For my mer - ry men and
first man that John Do - ry did meet Was good King John of
(4.) par - don, a par - don, my liege and king, For my mer - ry men and

19
John of France, King John
John of France, King John
France - a; John Do - ry could well of his cour - te - sie, But
me - a, And all the churls in mer - ry Eng - land, I'll
France - a; John Do - ry could well of his cour - te - sie, But
me - a, And all the churls in mer - ry Eng - land, I'll
22
p
of France, King John of
p
of France, King John of
p
fell down in a trance - a, but fell down in a
bring them bound to thee - a, I'll bring them bound to
p
fell down in a trance - a, but fell down in a
bring them bound to thee - a, I'll bring them bound to
p

25
1.
2.
p
div.
France, up - on a ho - ly France. 'And bring them
France, up - on a ho - ly France.
mf
5. And
trance - a.
4. 'A thee - a.'
f
trance - a, but fell down in a trance.
4. 'A thee - a, I'll bring them bound to
27
bound to thee.'
A
(6.) hoist their sails
They
Ni - chol was then a Corn - ish man, A lit - tle be - side Bo -
(6.) hoist their sails both top and top, The miz - en and all was
pp
A Corn - - - - - ish
They hoist their
thee.'
A Corn - ish
(6.) hoist
They hoist their

30
Corn - - - - - ish man,
hoist their sails,
- hyde - a, He manned a
tried - a; And each stood
f
man, And he manned forth a good black bark, With
sails, And ev - 'ry man stood to his lot, What
(pp)
man, He
sails, each
f
33
pp
He manned a
And each stood
good black bark, With fif - ty good oars on a
to his lot, What - ev - er should be -
fif - ty good oars on a side - a,
ev - er should be - tide - a,
manned a bark, With fif - ty good oars on a
stood to his lot, What - ev - er should be -

36
f
p
1.
2.
good black bark, With fif-ty good oars on a side. 6. They
to his lot, What-ev-er should be- -tide.
side-a, with fif-ty good oars on a side. 6. They
-tide-a, what-ev-er should be- -tide. 7. The
with fif-ty good oars on a side.
what-ev-er should be- -tide. Dub-a-dub
side, with fif-ty good oars on a side. 6. They
-tide, what-ev-er should be- -tide. 7. The
mf
ff
39
Dub-a-dub dub, dub-a-dub dub, dub-a-dub dub,
roar-ing can-non then were plied, And dub-a-dub went the
(8.) grap-pling hooks were brought at length, The brown bill and the
dub, dub-a-dub dub, dub-a-dub dub, dub-a-dub
roar-ing can-non then were plied, And dub-a-dub went the
(8.) grap-pling hooks were brought at length, The brown bill and the

42
dub - a-dub dub, The bray - ing trum - pets loud they cried To
John Do - ry at length, for all his strength, Was
drum - a, The bray - ing trum - pets loud they cried To
sword - a; John Do - ry at length, for all his strength, Was
dub, The bray - ing trum - pets loud they cried To
John Do - ry at length, for all his strength, Was
drum - a, The bray - ing trum - pets loud they cried To
sword - a; John Do - ry at length, for all his strength, Was
45
cou - rage all and some - a, to cou - rage all and
clapt fast un - der board - a, was clapt fast un - der
cou - rage all and some - a, to cou - rage all and
clapt fast un - der board - a, was clapt fast un - der
cou - rage all and some - a, to cou - rage all and
clapt fast un - der board - a, was clapt fast un - der
cou - rage all and some - - - - - - -
clapt fast un - der board - - - - - - -

48a
1.
some - a. Dub - a - dub
some - a. 8. The
some - a. to cou - rage all and some. Dub - a - dub
- - a a. 8. The
- - a a.
1.
rit.
48b
2.
board - a, was clapt fast un - der board.
board - a, was clapt fast un - der board.
board - a, was clapt fast un - der board.
- - a, was clapt fast un - der board.
rit.
2.

Nothing is here for tears

John Milton (adap.)
(1608–74)

RALPH VAUGHAN WILLIAMS (1872–1958)
arr. John Leavitt

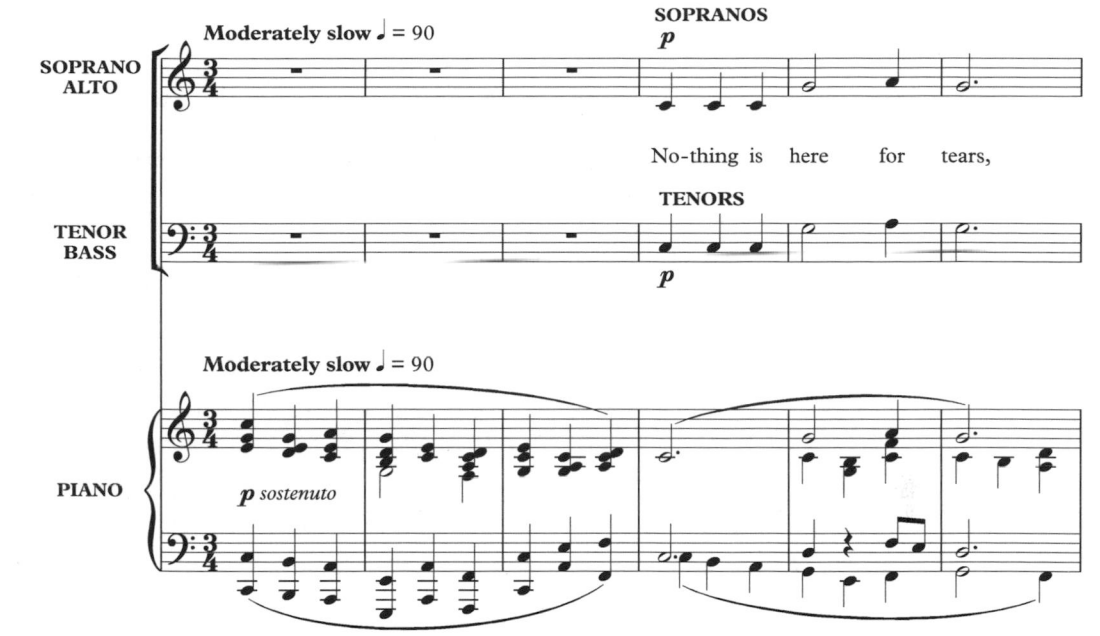

Duration: *c.*2 mins

© Oxford University Press 1936 & 2020

13
qui - et us in a death so no - ble.
18
ALTOS
p
Let us go fetch him hence, and so - lemn-ly at - tend, With si - lent
BASSES
p
24
A.
ob - se-quy and fu - ner-al train, Home to his fa - ther's house.
B.

31
S./A
T./B.
f risoluto
There will we build him a mo - nu-ment
f risoluto
f risoluto
36
With all his tro - phies hung, and acts en - rolled.
41
unis.
S.
A.
Thi - ther shall all the va - liant youth re-sort, And from his
unis.
T.
B.

46
ff
me - mo-ry in-flame their breasts To match-less va-lour
ff
ff
6
marcato
51
unis.
and ad-ven-tures high.
unis.

She's like the swallow

Newfoundland folksong
arr. RALPH VAUGHAN WILLIAMS (1872–1958)
arr. for SATB choir by John Leavitt

Duration: *c.*2 mins

This song is taken from *Folk Songs from Newfoundland*, collected and edited by Maud Karpeles.

© Oxford University Press 1934 & 2020

13
prim - e - rose; The more she plucked the more she pulled Un -
loo loo loo loo loo loo loo loo loo
loo loo loo loo loo
loo loo loo loo loo loo loo loo loo loo
16
-til she got her a - per - on full. loo
mf
loo loo loo loo loo loo loo loo loo.
It's
loo loo loo loo loo loo.
loo loo loo loo loo loo loo
mf
19
out of these ros - es she made a bed, A ston - y pil - low
22
dim.
for her head. She laid her down, no word did say, Un -
dim.

25
break.
mp
-til this fair maid's heart did break, her heart did break. She's
mp
28
like the swal-low that flies so high, She's like the riv-er that
31
SOLO mp
I
ne-ver runs dry, She's like the sun-shine on the lee shore, I
34
dim. e rit.
love my love and love is no more.
loo loo loo loo
p
love my love and love is no more.
loo loo loo loo
loo
loo loo
p

Greensleeves

English folksong
arr. RALPH VAUGHAN WILLIAMS (1872–1958)
arr. for SATB choir by John Leavitt

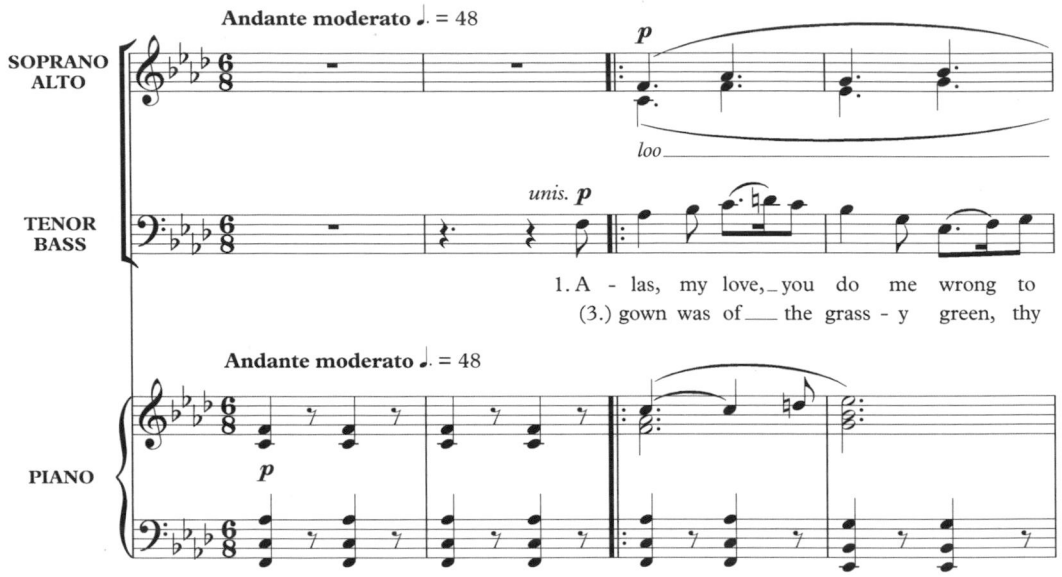

Duration: *c.*3 mins

© Oxford University Press 1934, 1945, 1954, & 2020

8
you so long, de - light - ing in your com - pa - ny.
har - vest queen, and yet thou would - est not love me.
11
mf
Green - sleeves was all my joy, Green - sleeves was
T.
B. mf
mf
14
my de - light, Green - sleeves was my heart of gold, and

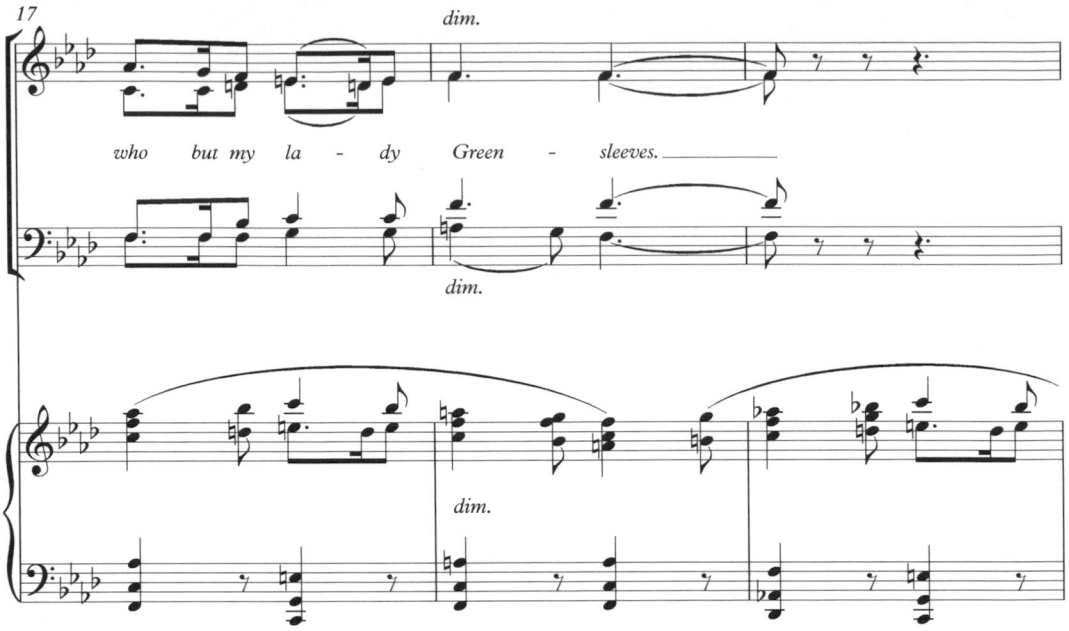
17
dim.
who but my la - dy Green - sleeves.
dim.
dim.

20
unis. mp
2. I have been read - y
4. Well, I will pray to
A - las, my
p
mp
2. I have been
4. Well, I will
mp

23
at your hand, to grant what - ev - er you would crave; I
God on high, that thou my con - stan - cy may'st see; For
love, a - las my love, my
read - y, read - - - y, I
pray, pray to God; For

26
have both wa - ged life and land, your love and good - will
I am still thy lov - er true; come once a - gain and
love, you do me wrong, you do me
have wa - ged life your good - will
I'm thy lov - er; come a - gain and

29
mf
for to have.
love me.
wrong.
Green - sleeves was all my joy,
for to have.
love me.
mf
mf

32
Green - sleeves was my de - light, Green - sleeves was my

35
dim.
heart of gold, and who but my la - dy Green - sleeves.
dim.
gold, my la - dy Green - sleeves.
dim.

1.
2.
38a
p
rit.
loo loo loo loo
unis. p
p
3. Thy loo loo loo loo
1.
2.
rit.
p
p

to the memory of
Charles Villiers Stanford, and his Blue Bird

Silence and Music

Ursula Wood
(1911–2007)

RALPH VAUGHAN WILLIAMS (1872–1958)
ed. John Leavitt

Duration: *c.*4 mins

© Oxford University Press 1953 & 2020

9
sleep - - ing swan, wings closed
pp
a sleep - ing swan, wings closed
pp
a sleep - ing swan, wings closed
pp
a sleep - ing swan, wings closed
12
and drift - ing where the wa - - ter leads, a
and drift - - ing, drift - ing,
and drift - - ing, drift - ing,
and drift - - ing, drift - ing,

15
win-ter moon, a grove where sha-dows dream, a
a win - ter moon, a grove where sha -
a win - ter moon, a grove where sha -
a win - ter moon, a grove where sha -
18
hand out-stretched to ga - ther hol - low reeds,
- dows dream, hol - - - low
- dows dream, hol - - - low
- dows dream, hol - - - low

22
hol - - - low reeds
reeds.
reeds.
reeds.
mf
The four winds in their
mf
25
p
The four winds
p
The four winds
p
The four winds
li - ta-nies can tell all of earth's sto-ries as they weep
p

28
weep and cry,
weep and cry,
weep and cry,
and cry, weep,
30
the sea names all the trea - sure of her
weep and cry, the sea names her
the sea names all the trea - sure of her
weep and cry, the sea names her

33
cresc.
f
tides, the birds re - joice, re - joice,
36
ff
re - joice, re-joice be - tween the earth and sky.

40
pp
più p
Voi - ces of grief and from the heart of joy; so near to
Voi - ces of grief and from the heart of joy; so near to
Voi - ces of grief and from the heart of joy; so near to
Voi - ces of grief and from the heart of joy; so near to
44
cresc.
com - pre-hen - sion do we stand that wind and sea and all of
com - pre-hen - sion do we stand that wind and sea and all of
com - pre - hen - sion do we stand that wind and sea and all of
com - pre-hen - sion do we stand that wind and sea and all of

48
winged de-light lie in the oc - taves of man's voice
winged de-light lie in the oc - taves of man's voice
winged de-light lie in the oc - taves of man's
winged de-light lie in the oc - taves of man's voice
52
and hand and mu - sic wakes,
and hand and mu - sic wakes
voice and hand and mu - sic wakes
of man's voice and hand and mu - sic wakes

56
p
pp
wakes from si - lence, from si - -
p
from si - - - lence,
p
from si - - - lence,
p
from si - - - lence,
p
pp
59
ppp niente
- - lence, si - lence, from si - lence, where it slept.
pp
from si - lence, where it slept.
pp
from si - lence, where it slept.
pp
from si - lence, where it slept.
ppp niente

Land of our birth

from 'A Song of Thanksgiving'

Rudyard Kipling
(1865–1936)

RALPH VAUGHAN WILLIAMS (1872–1958)
arr. for SATB choir by John Leavitt

Duration: c.5 mins

© Oxford University Press 1945 & 2020

12
S./A.
S./A. unis. p
2. Fa - ther in Heav'n who lov - est all, O help thy
16
chil - dren when they call, That they may build from age to
19
age An un - de - fil - ed he - ri - tage.
mf

23
unis. mf
S./A.
3. Teach us the strength that can - not seek, By deed or
unis.
T./B.
mf
26
thought to hurt the weak; That, un - der thee, we may pos -
29
-sess Man's strength to com-fort man's dis - tress.

32
p
4. Teach us de - light in sim - ple
4. Teach us de - light in sim - ple
p
4. Teach us sim - ple
p
35
things, The mirth that has no bit - ter springs; For - give - ness
things, The mirth that has no bit - ter springs; For - give - ness
things, no bit - - - ter springs; For - give - ness
38
free of e - vil done, And love to all men 'neath the
free of e - vil done, And love to all men 'neath the

41
sun.
sun.
f
45
unis. ff
5. Land of our birth, our faith, our pride, For whose dear
unis.
ff
ff
49
O Mo - ther-land we pledge to
sake our fa - thers died; O Mo - ther - land, we pledge to

53
thee, Head, heart and hand through the years
57
to be.